GETTING "YES" DECISIONS

What insurance agents and
financial advisors can say to clients.

BERNIE DE SOUZA & TOM "BIG AL" SCHREITER

Published by Fortune Network Publishing
PO Box 890084
Houston, TX 77289 USA
Telephone: +1 (281) 280-9800

ISBN-10: 1-892366-81-9
ISBN-13: 978-1-892366-81-8

Disclaimer.

Financial services and security laws vary from company to company, from region to region, and from country to country. This book does not render financial, investment, insurance or legal advice for the financial services or insurance profession. It is only a guide to help understand how we can communicate more effectively with our potential clients.

Advice fees, commissions, investment wording, etc. all must be done within the laws of our region or country. So please modify the scripts, ideas and advice in this book accordingly.

To make reading easier, we will use "he and his," instead of "he or she" and "his or her," etc. This just makes it faster to read. Please substitute the gender you feel is appropriate.

And finally, a special thanks to Andrew Stinchcomb for his technical help with this book.

Contents

The purpose of business is to solve people's problems.

There is no other reason for business to exist.

- If we owned a restaurant, and people never got hungry, that would be a terrible business.

- If we owned a hotel, and people never got sleepy, that would be a terrible business.

- If we sold life insurance, and people lived forever, that would be a terrible business.

- If we gave advice about investments, and people were currently wealthy beyond their wildest dreams, that would be a terrible business.

Unless people have problems, we don't have a business. We should celebrate that people have problems. The more problems they have, the more they need us!

So what kind of problems could our prospects have?

Here is a partial list to get us thinking:

- They might die too soon.

- They might die without an adequate financial plan.

- They might not have enough money for retirement.

- They don't want to spend years studying to become an investment expert.

- They don't want to read 2,000 pages of new tax laws every year.

- They want to make sure their children have enough money for university.

- They can't get ahead financially with low interest returns on their savings account.

- They can't save enough money to ensure their family will be cared for after their death.

- They don't understand the different types of life insurance.

- They don't have a will or estate plan.

- They don't know who to go to for competent financial advice.

- They need to guarantee their loan at the bank with life insurance.

- They hate complicated financial plans, and want something simple.

- They want to take advantage of tax incentives, but they don't know where to start.

- They want someone to provide a big picture of a financial plan, and for that someone to take care of the details.

- They want to feel good about their financial plans, but they don't know who to trust.

- They have a full-time career, and they don't have time to keep up with changes in financial legislation.

Lots of big problems.

There is no shortage of problems for our potential clients. And of course, they want to fix their problems.

We can help. But only if we get our potential clients to make a "yes" decision to move forward.

Educating our potential clients is useless for them, unless they take action. Education without taking action … is the same as no education.

Our job is to get potential clients to take action to fix their problems.

I have a mystery.

Two financial advisors join a firm.

Both financial advisors:

- Have the same background.

- Know the same prospects.

- Have the same motivation.

- Set the same goals.

- Work the same hours.

- Make the same number of phone calls.

- Present to the same people.

Yet, one advisor fails, while the other advisor enjoys massive success.

Why?

What was the difference?

The answer.

The first advisor talked and presented to his potential clients. Based upon the words he chose, his potential clients made a decision not to do business with him.

The second advisor talked and presented to his potential clients. Based upon the different words he chose, those same potential clients made a decision to do business with him.

The words we choose will affect our potential clients' decisions.

We can buy impressive chairs, a mahogany desk, get certificates and diplomas, but ultimately, our prospects make decisions based on the words we say.

A decision?

Yes.

Unless a prospect makes a decision to move forward, everything will stay the same. The prospect will continue to have the same unsolved problems in his life.

And, that is our job. To help our prospects make a decision to solve their problems.

How do prospects make up their minds?

We can network, create prospects, set appointments, conduct seminars, and give presentations.

That is nice. This might make us feel good, and maybe entertain our prospects.

But unless our prospects make a decision to buy from us or engage our services, we are not in business.

And that is the whole story.

We are in the "decision-making" business. We have to get prospects to make decisions to:

- Take our phone calls.

- Set an appointment.

- Believe what we say.

- Listen to us.

- Do business with us!

Our real profession is getting decisions.

Once we know that we are in the decision business, everything gets clearer. We won't stress about how in-depth the annuity tables are, rewrite investment disclaimers, micro-analyze premiums, or create laminated proposals. All of these things come later. Our first task is getting the "yes" decision from our prospects.

How does that work in real life?

What are our prospects thinking when they meet us?

Let's look inside their brains and see what's happening.

Step #1: "Who are you?"

Step #2: "Can I trust you?"

Step #3: "Am I interested in what you say?"

Step #4: "Do I want it or not?"

Step #5: "If I want it, okay, give me the details."

As we noticed above, "Give me the details" is the presentation part of our business. This is where we show the various solutions, the reports, the needs analysis, etc.

This comes last!

Yes, as we shall soon see, most prospects actually make their final decision to do business with us or not ... before they even see our presentation!

Hard to believe?

Hold on. Don't panic. We will get to some fascinating case studies of how quickly prospects make decisions. But before that, let's take a peek at the big decision.

Why do our clients choose us instead of our competition?

Why our clients desperately need us.

Imagine our client went to university to become an engineer. After four years of university, our client invested in additional courses to get more qualifications. Maybe our client invested six or seven years into an engineering education.

At this point, our client feels confident about engineering. And he should.

- But what about insurance?

- What about investing?

- What about investment vehicles that may have unique tax-saving advantages?

Is our client an expert in these areas?

Of course not. And that is why clients need us.

The average client has time for his career, his family, and possibly a bit of free time for a hobby. Our client certainly can't invest another four or seven years to become an expert in insurance or investments.

So what can the client do?

The sensible option is to find a trusted advisor to help sort through the hundreds or even thousands of options. That advisor should be us.

Our client lacks enough information to pick the appropriate insurance or investments. Why?

#1. No formal education or training in that area.

#2. No time to keep up with the yearly changes. The tax implications for certain investments require research and reading several hundred pages of new information every year.

#3. No experience in this area. Without experience, how can the client evaluate long-term or short-term trends?

An amateur, with limited resources and information, could make completely inappropriate insurance and investment decisions.

That is where we come in. We can narrow down the options. We can help a client focus on his financial goals. We can offer suggestions and options that a client may not be aware of.

So why will the client choose us?

Let's see how this choice is made from the viewpoint of a typical client.

Our potential client sets an appointment for his initial consultation. Nervous, he arrives at our office, sits down, and begins to explain his problem.

Now, this potential client can describe his problem to one hundred different financial advisors. The problem remains the same. Which advisor should he choose to help solve his problem?

So why does this potential client choose us? Or rather, how does he make the decision to not choose any one of the other 99 financial advisors? What is the potential client looking at?

- Our expensive furniture?

- Our academic credentials and certificates on our wall?

- The size of our office?

- If the free tea or coffee was tasty?

- If our chairs were soft and comfortable?

- The biased testimonials on our website?

- The fine art and pictures on our wall?

- If our suit appears custom-tailored?

- Our commanding, pompous voice?

- The courtesy of reception?

- The cute graphics in our ad?

- Our all-knowing nodding when they explain their financial situation?

- Our description of our discounted fees?

- The payment plan?

- The style of our business card?

Unless we understand how prospects make their final decision, we will continue to miss potential business.

What does all this mean?

We have to "close." We must get a "yes" decision from our prospects.

Does that sound challenging or uncomfortable? It could. Especially if we use untrained, ugly sales techniques of the past.

Want to see why prospects hate pushy salesmen that try to close them to make a decision?

Why closing doesn't work.

How does traditional closing work?

The advisor carefully grinds through his pre-planned presentation facts, features, benefits, and calls to action. To get to the final decision, the advisor might use soft closing questions such as:

- "So what did you like most about the presentation?"

- "Is there anything that might prevent you from moving forward?"

- "So how do you feel about this?"

- "How do you see this fitting into your plan?"

Or, the advisor might use hard closing questions or statements such as:

- "So, shall we get started?"

- "Should we activate the application now, or would tomorrow be better?"

- "Let's start filling in the paperwork now."

Or, an out-of-touch, rude advisor might even say:

- "What is it going to take to get you to start this plan today?"

- "Don't you love your family?"

- "Any adult can see this makes sense. So what is holding you back?"

Yes, something doesn't feel right. We gave a quality presentation, covered each important benefit, and summarized our offer. Yet, we still feel guilty and hesitant trying to close at the end of our presentation.

Why?

Because we are closing at the **wrong time!**

Can you figure out this next mystery?

Some agents and financial advisors earn a fortune.

Others never make it in the business.

Hmmm.

Same territory. Same prospects. Same economy. Same portfolio of offerings. Same sales meetings. Same goals.

Sure, some people have more contacts. Others may have more skills or better backgrounds. And yet others may just work harder. But this isn't the whole story.

What we are looking for is the big secret.

We want the "Aha!" moment that will quickly take us to the top levels of our profession. We want the key to the universe of closing prospects easily, with no rejection and no stress.

Is there a big secret? Yes.

Is it obvious? No.

Now, we could tell you the secret, but you wouldn't believe it.

This "Aha!" moment is so weird, so against everything that we believe, that it is almost impossible for us to believe it when we first hear it.

We have to experience this "Aha!" moment.

We have to come to our own conclusion that this "Aha!" moment is real.

Are you ready to experience this "Aha!" moment?

13 case studies to change your career.

Let's take a look at how humans make decisions. Observe the following case studies closely.

See how many case studies we have to read … before we get that "Aha!" moment.

Ready?

Case study #1:

We go online to watch a video on YouTube. How many seconds does it take for us to make our final decision if we want to watch that video or not? Five seconds? Ten seconds? In just a few seconds we make our final decision whether we want to watch that video or not. We make our final decision before we actually see the video!

Case study #2:

We are hungry. We walk past a restaurant and decide to go inside to eat. We make our final decision to eat at this restaurant before we even see the menu!

Case study #3:

We browse the menu at the restaurant. Something catches our eye and we decide to order that entrée. But how much information do we have about that entrée? Were the vegetables organically grown? Did the chicken live a happy life before it was killed? We don't know. However, we made our final decision to purchase that entrée without a fact-filled presentation. Hmmm.

Case study #4:

Have we ever received a telephone call from a salesman? How many seconds into the telephone call before we make our final decision? Most times we make a "no" decision before the salesman finishes his first sentence. We make our final decision before the presentation even starts! And guess what?

If we make our final decision with a salesman over the telephone in just a second or two, don't we think our prospects will do the same to us? What percentage of the time? Almost 100%.

Case study #5:

Let's go grocery shopping. We push our cart down aisle one. On the left is a box of corn flakes. Do we stop our cart, pick up the box of corn flakes and read the nutrition label? Do we check to see the background of the company founder? Do we review the financials of the cornflake company? Do we consider the lost opportunity cost of eating cornflakes rather than doing some productive work?

No. We make an instant decision to bypass the cornflakes and continue down the aisle. If we had to stop and consider every item in the aisle, and get a full presentation on each item, we would starve before we reached the end of the first aisle.

Instead, how do we proceed down that grocery store aisle? We do this. Mentally we say, "No. No. No. Yes to that chocolate bar. No. No. Yes to that cake. No. No."

It appears we have pre-made decisions on almost every item in the grocery store.

Case study #6:

Imagine someone comes up to us and says, "I just took my first lesson to become a chiropractor. I learned a brand-new technique on how to twist your neck. Want to be first?"

How quick was our decision? In one second, we made our final decision. We think, "No. I want to survive. This sounds too dangerous. No. No. No." We made that immediate decision before we heard the details of the presentation. Before we heard that he saw this technique on the Internet. Before he told us 30% of the people could recover. Before he showed us some computer printouts.

Case study #7:

What if someone came up to us and said, "Can I take your children skydiving with me?" Now depending on what our children did to us while they were growing up, we would think, "Oh no. Please don't take my babies skydiving!" or "I would help push them out of the plane!" Assuming we love our children, our immediate answer would be, "No." How long did it take us to make that decision? It was instant. We have an internal program called "love of family."

Isn't it interesting that we made our final decision before he even started his skydiving presentation? Before he told us that he was a professional skydiver? Before he told us that he was successful three out of four times? Before he told us that we are only going to dive one centimeter? Yes, we make decisions before the details and the presentation.

Case study #8:

In ten days, the leader of the opposing political party is set to give a speech. He will address our nation on how he is going to fix all the current problems. Now, have we already made a decision? Have we already decided it will just be some political gibberish and fluff from the opposing political party's twisted viewpoint?

Of course. But think about this. We made our final decision about his speech instantly, but he won't even begin his speech for ten more days!

We definitely make our final decisions way before the facts and figures begin.

Case study #9:

We call a potential client and set an appointment for Tuesday at 10 AM. On Tuesday, our potential client does not show up to the appointment.

Has our potential client made a decision? Yes. He made a "no" decision. And the potential client made this decision based upon how much information? None.

And if our potential client does show up to the appointment, we know he has already made a decision to buy. Why? Because he made a decision to leave work, skip his coffee break, and to take time out of his busy day to meet with us.

Again, the decision to buy, the decision to do business with us, was made before the appointment. The potential client made his "yes" or "no" decision before the presentation and information.

Case study #10:

The ladies' shoe store. A lady walks into a large shoe store. Over 1,000 pairs of ladies' shoes on display. But next door is a ladies' shoe store with a 95%-off sale!

How long will the lady stay in the original shoe store? Seconds.

The lady will make an instant "no" decision on 1,000 pairs of ladies' shoes, just so that she can run to the next store with that incredible 95%-off sale.

Notice that this lady did not receive a single presentation on the original 1,000 pairs of shoes. No salesman told her about the quality of the Italian leather, about the little old shoemaker who lived up in the mountains, that the shoemaker's son walked with a crutch, the reinforced shoe buckles, the history of the styling, how someone cut the original leather from a favorite cow's hide, etc.

Case study #11:

A man sits in front of the television mindlessly channel-surfing. The remote control goes, "Click. Click. Click. Click." After two seconds of viewing a channel, the man changes to the next channel. This behavior drives women crazy. Women say, "How can he make a decision to watch that channel? He hasn't even seen anything yet! Men are so stupid!" But, the man makes the final decision to continue surfing channels until he makes a "yes" decision on a channel that instantly interests him.

Case study #12:

At live workshops, I ask this question of the ladies. "Ladies, have you ever, sometime in your lifetime, met a young man, made up your mind about that young man, and where that young man would fit into your life, and made that decision within the first 30 seconds of meeting that young man?"

And the answer is, "Yes."

Then I asked the men at the workshop, "Is this fair?"

Of course the men agree this is not fair. The ladies have

not heard the men's presentations yet! But, this is how it works in real life. The ladies made the decision way **before** the presentation begins.

Case study #13:

At the same live workshop, I ask this question of the entire audience. "How many people here have made their final decision to enter a relationship before they had all the information?"

After some uncomfortable laughs, the audience agrees that we make our final decisions almost instantly. The information does not come until much later.

Are we starting to see a trend?

So what do all these case studies mean to me?

Get ready for it.

Here it comes.

We don't want to hear this …

But based upon these 13 case studies, here is the obvious conclusion.

Potential clients make their final "yes" or "no" decision … almost instantly.

They don't make decisions after our presentation.

They make decisions **BEFORE** our presentation.

This is so important to our career. The decision to buy or to do business with us comes first!

What we do in the first 30 seconds is everything. This is when the prospect decides:

Step #1. "Who are you?"

Step #2. "Can I trust you?"

Step #3. "Am I interested in what you say?"

Step #4. "Do I want to do business with you or not?"

30 seconds! This all happens so fast.

Our business is getting the "yes" decision because that is what we are paid to do.

Only after we take care of Step #4: Do I want to do business with you or not? ... then, and only then, do we proceed to:

Step #5: "If I want it, okay, give me the details."

This is the step where we explain the details of how our plan will work for our new client. This could include:

- A follow-up fact-finding interview.

- Scheduling a presentation with the potential client and his accountant.

- PowerPoint presentations.

- Charts.

- Amortization tables.

- Research reports.

- Customized client proposals.

- Regulatory disclaimers.

- Contracts and forms.

- Payment options.

- Past performance of investments.

- Company finances and ratings.

- Future trend and inflation projections.

Tell me again about Step #5.

The actual presentation can happen on the first visit, or during later visits when we need to present complex research and reports. There is no Step #5 if the prospect makes a decision against us or our possible solutions to his problem.

We only want to talk to potential clients who make a "yes" decision.

Wouldn't it be easier if everyone we presented to had already made a "yes" decision in their minds? Then, every fact and figure of our presentation will be exciting to them.

No sales resistance, no skepticism, no rejection.

This is the "Aha" moment???

Yes. The first 30 seconds of decisions will define our career.

If the potential client makes a "no" decision in the first 30 seconds, we are finished. Done. It is over.

There is no need to torture the prospect with 45 more minutes of facts and figures, or with embarrassing probing questions. We don't have to make endless callbacks and follow-ups. We can stop harassing the prospect immediately.

Our prospect made a decision not to believe us, not to trust us, or is just not interested … so let's be polite. Let's take the hint. Let's move on to potential clients who want our services.

But what if it is just not the right time for our prospect?

Maybe their circumstances will change in the future.

Perhaps. This can be part of our follow-up that we do for our business. However, we are not paid for follow-up. We get paid for getting "yes" decisions.

So we focused this book on our primary mission, to get "yes" decisions from our potential clients.

For goal-setting, personal development, financial education, professional skill development, sending out holiday and birthday cards, perpetual follow-up, sales meetings conduct, licensing requirements, regulatory disclaimers, and other duties ... there are other books and resources for that part of our career.

Now this brings up an interesting question.

Let's get back to decisions.

The obvious interesting question would be, "How much information does the human brain need to make a final decision?"

It appears to be: none.

Isn't it interesting that we make up our minds before the presentation even starts? As professionals, we must realize that our prospects' decisions are not based on the plan, the products, the return on investment, the guarantee, or the life expectancy tables.

Prospects base their decisions on how we start!

Is this fair?

Of course not. But it is simply how it works.

Final decisions are quick.

There is an old saying, "We only get one chance to make a good first impression." There is a lot of truth in that statement.

We have to manage the first few seconds of our presentations efficiently and professionally. Why? Because that is when and where our potential clients make their final decisions.

Skeptical? Of course. This may not feel right based upon our previous beliefs. But changing this belief could be the breakthrough we need to excel in our profession.

Ready for some real-life examples of how quickly our potential clients make decisions? And how our clients make decisions based upon no presentation or information?

Five opening words.

I look like a salesman. I act like a salesman. I smell like a salesman. And I come up to you and I start my conversation with these five words:

"Would you be interested in … ?"

Have you made a decision? Yes.

After just five words, the voice in the back of your mind is screaming, "Salesman! Run, run, save yourself! Hide your wallet! Hide your purse! Shields up! Salesman approaching! Think of excuses!"

Wow. After just five words our minds make an instant "no" decision based on a stored program. We call this stored program the "salesman alarm."

Prospects instantly activate this program when they hear, "Would you be interested in … ?" From that moment on, the potential client will be skeptical, sales-resistant, and negative. Why? Because his mind has already made the final decision.

We are dead.

Now, it doesn't matter if we set goals, have a vision board, chant affirmations, or just have a positive outlook on life. If we say these five words, it can be over in seconds.

Prospects respond to what we say. They make their final decisions very quickly. Why?

Because the human brain has to make thousands of decisions every second.

We don't have time to think everything over, every time. We've seen some of these need-to-make-every-second decisions before. So our mind says, "Hey, if we see that same set of circumstances again, here is the automatic decision we will make. No thinking. Just activate this decision."

Thousands of decisions? Yes. Every second. Our brains suffer from decision-overload.

Let's look at just a few of the decisions our minds make in just one second.

- Check to see if we are thirsty.

- Pump blood to the muscles in our right thigh.

- Create 30,000 new digestive enzymes.

- See if that movement to our right is dangerous.

- Is the person sitting next to me wearing a scary hockey mask and carrying an ax?

- Keep our balance.

- Coordinate 13 muscles to make a smile.

- Ignore that loud noise over there.

- Blink our eyes.

- Adjust our body temperature.

- Add more clothing because we feel cold.

- Is that person I see moving towards me or away from me?

- Tilt my body a bit forward as I am falling backwards slightly.

- The squirrel across the street is not interesting.

- Time to make my heart beat again.

- Don't pay attention to that siren.

- Step back from that speeding car.

- Good idea to scratch my shoulder now.

- Left foot ... then ... the right foot. Don't break this walking pattern.

This is only a partial list. But as we can see, the thinking part of our human brain cannot keep up. So here is what our brain does to adjust.

It keeps a list of "stored decisions."

Our minds have "stored" decisions?

What does this mean?

This means we don't have to re-think every situation. We don't have time for that. So we make up our minds about things based upon past experiences. Then we store that decision for future use.

Here is a perfect example. We trip over broken pavement. Our face rapidly approaches the ground. We have a stored decision to put up our hands to protect our face.

Where did we get that stored decision? From when we learned to walk. After several falling-on-our-face experiences, we formed a program. Now when we fall forward, this program immediately activates certain muscles to throw up our hands and arms to protect our face.

Now, if we didn't have that program, things would be ugly. We trip. We observe the ground rapidly approaching our face. We use our conscious mind to think, "Oh wow. This isn't right. This could hurt. Maybe I should activate muscle #1 in my right arm to start a sequence of muscles to start bending my arms forward. Yeah. That sounds right. Oh wait, I could do that with my other arm too. And then I should…" Splat!

Our conscious mind takes way too long to make decisions. We don't have time for that. Our day is way too busy every second.

Here are some examples of stored decisions.

- Chocolate. We liked it before, and we want it again. When someone offers us chocolate, we immediately say, "Sure."

- Salesmen. Run! Run! Save ourselves. Why? Because they talk forever. They won't leave until we give them money. They won't listen. Because of previous bad experiences, we store a decision to avoid salesmen.

- Politicians. They will say anything to get elected. Don't believe every campaign promise.

- I like comedies. Or, I like adventure movies.

- Exercise is hard and it hurts.

- I don't trust people with beards.

- Jump and panic when I see mice.

- Don't push that fork too far inside my mouth.

We have hundreds of thousands or even millions of stored decisions that operate our lives. It is like we are on autopilot. Our stored decisions carry us through life, while we have brief moments of conscious thought.

If decisions are pre-made, then we don't need information to make our decisions.

In most situations in life, we already have made our final decision.

So what decisions might our prospects pre-make?

- To protect their family.

- To not trust strangers.

- To be wealthy.

- To treat telephone calls as interruptions.

- To avoid risk.

- To be skeptical of three-piece suits and ties.

- To refuse to meet with salespeople.

- To make excuses and lie to avoid appointments.

- To stick their head in the sand and hope papers with complex numbers go away.

- To get the best returns on investments.

- To avoid making a decision because friends might make fun of their choice.

- To delay and put off decisions for fear of being wrong.

Yes, most decisions are pre-made.

Information won't change those decisions. Using our presentations to get decisions just won't work.

No information needed for decisions?

Sounds weird, but let's look at a few more case studies.

Case study #1:

Overweight people. They have books, brochures, audios, weight-loss clinics, exercise studios, diet drinks, protein powders, herbal fat burners, appetite suppressants ... they have been preached to, lectured, sent articles from the Internet ... every overweight person in the universe got the **information**.

Ask any overweight person in the universe, "How do you lose weight?"

They will answer, "Two things. First, eat less food. And second, exercise more."

Every overweight person in the universe got the information.

So if humans made decisions based on information ... there would be no more overweight people!

But are there overweight people? Yes.

Will you see overweight people everywhere you go? Yes.

Was any of this overweight-reducing information used in their decisions? Obviously not.

Case study #2:

Remember talking about political candidates earlier in this book? Imagine we are a member of a conservative party.

The leader of the opposing liberal party starts a speech. How long does it take us to make up our minds? From the moment the leader of the opposing party begins the speech we are thinking, "Liar! Liar! Not true! Not true!"

Or, what if the leader of the opposing party makes the following claim? He says, "I am going to improve the lives of our citizens with my powerful new initiatives. I will outline my entire plan at next week's convention."

Have we already made up our minds? Yes. We instantly decide this is going to be the stupidest speech in the history of civilization. But notice this. Just like earlier in this book, we made our final decision on this speech before it was even over!

No information was needed for us to make this decision. In fact, we made our final decision before the information was even presented.

Case study #3:

Show 100 people our presentation. The same information to 100 people. Now, if people made decisions on information, that would mean that either 100% would do business with us, or 100% would not do business with us. They all saw the same information.

But that's not true. Some people will do business with us, and some won't. Yet they all see the same information. So wouldn't it occur to us that people are making decisions on something other than information? Hmmm.

Case study #4:

We sit down with a prospect. He folds his arms. He leans far back in his chair. He frowns.

Has this prospect made a decision about us and our services? Yes.

And what was that decision? "No."

And how much information did the prospect receive so far? Zero.

Case study #5:

We call a prospect to get an appointment. The prospect says, "I am not interested in what you offer." His decision? "No."

And how much information did our prospect have about what we offer? Zero.

Disturbing. But obvious.

Based upon just our observations, here is the bottom line.

1. Prospects make their final decision based on zero information.

2. Prospects make their final decision immediately, before the presentation begins.

Sad, but true.

We hoped that our finely-tuned sales presentation would make a difference.

So how do we feel about our sales presentation now? In most cases, it's a total waste of time (for getting decisions). Our sales presentation usually has nothing to do with our prospect's final decision.

Yes, there will be exceptions. Extremely analytical prospects will insist on a complete blow-by-blow description of every feature. However, consider this.

These extremely analytical prospects already made a decision to do business with us. Why else would they even be talking with us now? All they want is enough data to satisfy their analytical needs. They want to make sure that our product or service will solve their problem. They want to justify their pre-made decision.

What about all the mandatory disclaimers required by regulators? Yes, we will have to do these disclaimers in our presentation. But, they are not part of the decision-making process.

Remember, the presentation is Step #5, after the prospect makes that mental decision to do business with us. This is the perfect place for all the probing questions, data presenting, disclaimers, etc. All of these things work better after the potential client decides they want to do business with us.

Should this change how we work?

Yes.

Based upon our observation of the human experience, what will we do differently?

We will want to get the final decision ... **before** we start our presentation.

Think of the possibilities. If we get a final "yes" decision before our presentation:

#1. We won't have to sell.

#2. We won't have objections.

#3. We won't have to use facts and data to convince prospects.

#4. We can relax and answer any questions our prospects have.

#5. Our presentations will be short.

#6. Our audience will be prospects who have already made a mental "yes" decision.

This is getting easier.

Back to those five ugly words.

Do you remember those five words, "Would you be interested in … ?"

Do you remember how those five words got an instant "no" decision in our prospects' minds? Well, before we move on, let's do something about those words.

Changing just a few words can be the difference between success and failure. Our careers may hinge on just a few words. Scary.

Try and identify the feeling you get when I ask you these questions:

- "Would you be interested in giving me an appointment?"

- "Would you be interested in meeting to discuss your financial options?"

- "Would you be interested in buying more insurance?"

- "Would you be interested in investing through me?"

- "Would you be interested in reviewing your retirement plan with me?"

Do you get the "no" feeling after hearing these questions?

Why? Because the phrase, "Would you be interested in … ?" activates the stored "no" decision in prospects' minds.

What would happen if we changed these five words slightly? Could a new five-word phrase activate a stored "yes" decision in our prospects' minds?

Yes, our prospects' behavior and decisions can change drastically by just changing a few words. Here is the new five-word phrase that we will use:

"Would it be okay if … ?"

Here is what happens when we say, "Would it be okay if … ?" This phrase will activate a different stored decision in our prospects' minds. They will be thinking:

- "That was a very polite way to ask."

- "Because you were polite, I feel obligated to say 'yes' immediately."

- "I want to help you any way I can, as long as your request is reasonable."

- "I feel good that you are asking for my help."

Want to feel the difference?

Here are some examples:

- "Would it be okay if we met for lunch on Friday?"

- "Would it be okay if we spent 30 minutes arranging a better retirement plan for you?"

- "Would it be okay if I advised you of the appropriateness of three different accumulation strategies?"

- "Would it be okay if I spent 20 minutes with you to give you a proper financial plan?"

- "Would it be okay if you could have a higher retirement income, without having to invest more money?"

- "Would it be okay if the government helped fund your retirement plan?"

- "Would it be okay if we could keep your insurance costs low?"

- "Would it be okay if you could protect your family without investing a fortune?"

- "Would it be okay if I could help some of your friends also?"

- "Would it be okay if I spent 20 minutes explaining all the new tax laws for your retirement plan? And that way you won't have to spend one week trying to figure it out?"

- "Would it be okay if you could get a better return on your pension fund?"

- "Would it be okay if you could use some of your income tax money for your retirement plan, instead of giving it to the government?"

- "Would it be okay if you took advantage of the latest tax incentives for small businesses?"

- "Would it be okay if you had a simple financial plan so that you could sleep well at night?"

- "Would it be okay if you could retire ten years earlier by simply rearranging your investments?"

- "Would it be okay if we make your savings and investments safer, so you wouldn't have to worry about risk?"

- "Would it be okay if we research the major companies to get the lowest life insurance rate we can?"

Now, what do you feel in the back of your mind with this phrase, "Would it be okay if ... ?" Do you feel the automatic "yes" decision?

Just by changing a few words, there is a different feeling in our prospects' minds.

Now, will these opening words change over time? Possibly. What sounded good in the 1970s might sound dated today.

Here is the important lesson. We can observe which phrases work, and which don't work. Then, we will adjust our opening words and the first 30 seconds of conversation. Now we can get the maximum results.

So the secret is ...

Our prospects make their final decision in the first few moments. Doesn't it make sense for us to carefully manage the words we say in those first few moments?

There are two parts to this instant decision strategy.

Part One:
We must avoid word phrases that have a very low chance of acceptance. We might want to avoid phrases such as:

- "Would you be interested in ... ?"

- "Can I ... ?"

Part Two:
We need to form the habit of saying more acceptable phrases such as:

"Would it be okay if ... ?"

This will greatly increase our chances for success for almost any request we make.

Words make the difference.

The difference between "Would you be interested in ... ?" and "Would it be okay if ... ?" shows that we must be careful with our first words. In each of the five steps, our potential clients will be making some decisions.

So now what do we do?

Remember that mind-reading exercise we did at the beginning of this book? We looked into our prospects' minds and watched them decide:

Step #1: "Who are you?"

Step #2: "Can I trust you?"

Step #3: "Am I interested in what you say?"

Step #4: "Do I want it or not?"

Step #5: "If I want it, okay, give me the details."

Well, we don't have to worry much about Step #5: "If I want it, okay, give me the details." That is the easy part. And that only comes if we get a "yes" decision in our prospects' minds.

Remember, we don't want to be rude and force a presentation on a prospect. We only present if that prospect decides to do business with us first. Presentations come later, much later.

The first four steps are the most critical. These steps will define our career.

So let's go through these steps one at a time.

Competency in each of the five steps is easy.

Why? Because we already know the questions in our prospects' minds. Their questions are simple and to the point. This allows us to have honest conversations and relationships.

Sound like fun?

Let's take a look at the first criteria potential clients use to choose who should represent them.

Step #1: "Who are you?"

Yes, it matters who we are.

- Are we a stranger cold-calling?

- Someone who just walked off the street?

- Are we perceived as the worthless brother-in-law?

- Do they look at us with respect?

- Do they think we see them as a commission or advisor fee?

- Do they see us as a respected source of good advice and resources?

- Is this our first contact with the potential client?

- Have we been in touch with this person regularly?

- Were we recommended by his boss?

Prospects make instant judgments, so we'd better make sure our first impressions are good. We want our prospects to feel like they know us, and most importantly, respect us.

"We can't redesign our past."

Many years ago, my friend, Tim Browne, told me, "We can't redesign our past." Certainly true.

There is no option to change our past. The option of living in the future is impossible. That leaves us with … today. That is the only thing within our control.

Let's take a look at a few things that we can do so that prospects see us in a better light. Remember, we want them to not only know us, but to respect us.

1. Personal development.

There is an old saying, "Dogs know who to bite."

In other words, prospects sense insecurity and incompetency, and can tell if we are authentic.

So the question is, "Can we improve ourselves internally?"

Of course.

There is another old saying that goes like this: "Who you are speaks so loudly that I cannot hear what you are saying."

Let's ask ourselves, "Who do potential clients want to do business with? People who are generally negative, or people who are generally positive?"

The answer is obvious. The more positive our outlook towards life and the world, the more prospective clients we will attract. People don't go to parties to socialize with negative people. No one likes hearing other people complain.

It is easy to pick up a negative bias towards things. Just read the newspaper, listen to the news, or spend a few minutes with complaining friends. Our subconscious mind records all this negativity. We need to balance this daily negativity with some positive daily input.

What is a quick fix or way to improve our positive outlook on life? Well, we could read inspirational and motivational books. However, we are already busy with our careers and we don't have extra free time. Here is a simpler solution.

Listen to audio recordings.

Think about our morning. The alarm goes off on our phone. We press the stop button. What if we immediately pressed a button to start playing an inspirational, motivational, skill-improving or attitude-improving audio? This audio recording could be playing in the background while we shower and get ready for the day. No extra time taken out of our day. The input was automatic.

This is an easy habit that takes no willpower or effort.

People "sense" our viewpoints and beliefs. This is part of their judgment of us.

2. Building a reputation of service.

There are givers and takers. Givers attract people. People celebrate when takers leave the room.

Should we be a giver only so that we can attract more clients? Of course not. That would be shallow. It is okay to be a giver just because it is the right thing to do.

Our world is populated by takers. People feel entitled and complain about any unfairness. When we decide to be a giver, we separate ourselves from the mass of humanity. People notice. Prospective clients notice.

Having an attitude of service helps define who we are.

We take for granted all the resources and knowledge we have as insurance agents or financial advisors. We know a great deal about insurance, equities, and the opportunities in the financial markets. Just sharing this knowledge willingly with others qualifies us as a giver.

What do we have with a high perceived value for our potential clients? Let's make a partial list. I am sure you can come up with an extended list.

- Tax-saving ideas.

- Budgeting ideas.

- Ways to save money.

- Latest business developments.

- Where to find a lawyer.

- Where to find a good accountant.

- Where to get good tax preparation.

- Where to find a good real estate agent.

- How to make ordinary expenses tax-deductible.

- Great books.

- Estate tax savings ideas.

- Forms and lists.

- Investment comparisons.

- Retirement options.

It is easy to become a trusted resource of valuable information. Everyone loves a giver.

And yes, we can give in other ways also. Volunteering, charity work, committee work, etc. All are noticed by our potential clients.

Having an attitude of service to others is a character trait that everyone will notice.

3. Networking.

The more we network, the more exposure we have. Common sense. Here are just a few areas where networking will expand our footprint into the market.

First, networking groups. While most members of the networking group may not be our ideal prospects, they all have qualified contacts outside of the group. For example, the average person knows 200 people. We might only want to talk to five out of their 200 contacts. Those five contacts might be the most ideal prospects for our services.

Our strategy is to educate the members of our networking group. Not sell to them. Educate.

We don't educate the members with all of the knowledge we have accumulated. Instead, we choose one or two simple problems that we solve. Then, when a member recognizes a contact with this problem, he can easily recommend us.

Second, referrals. Good referral techniques are essential to our career. Many professionals use referrals only. Just as in networking groups, we have to prepare a simple script, a very short sales story, or describe a problem. We can't expect others to understand and explain our business on their own.

There are plenty of books and courses dedicated to this one topic - referrals.

Third, centers of influence. These are unique individuals that possess trust and influence with others. Specifically, we want to locate those who have trust and influence with our ideal prospects. We will spend a lot of time building, educating, and nurturing this relationship.

Again, this book is not about prospecting. This book is about getting **decisions** from our prospects.

However, unless people perceive us in a good light, we won't pass Step #1: "Who are you?"

But what about advertising?

Quick answer. How do you feel about the difference between an advertising message ... and a recommendation from a friend? Obviously, recommendations are more powerful. Advertising activates the salesman alarm and now our prospect is on the defensive.

But what about buying leads? The same quick answer. Leads will activate the prospects' salesman alarm before we make our first communication.

What is less important to my potential client's decision to do business with us?

Degrees, awards, and fancy initials after our name may look important to us. However, our potential clients are more concerned with their connection with us.

Getting awarded for being a C.P.S. (Certified Professional Student) might be important for other parts of our career. But for decisions? For that initial question of, "Who are you?" No.

Our educational initials are not nearly as important as the personal development, building a reputation of service, and networking that we do.

We don't need to spend much time on the question, "Who are you?"

This is pretty basic. Instead, we need to acknowledge the "elephant in the room." The biggest and most important question our prospects have is, "Can I trust you?"

So let's get on to this important question. This question will make the biggest difference in our career.

Step #2: "Can I trust you?"

Prospects don't want to do business with a business card. They want to do business with a real person. Only a few analytical prospects will do their own financial planning online. And this is only after months of study and comparison.

When our prospects feel safe about who we are, what do they want to know next?

"Can I trust you and trust what you are saying?"

This is the hardest, yet most important question we have to answer.

Decisions. Remember them?

How will our prospect make the decision to trust us and believe what we say?

Will our prospect think this? "Oh, you are just a salesman trying to earn money from my business. Everything you say will be biased." In that case, we are dead.

Or will our prospect think this? "You are going to promote whatever earns you the most money. I'd better be skeptical about your advice." Again, we are dead.

We cause this. How?

Here is just one way we lose our prospect's trust.

By jumping into the presentation and solution, way before the prospect has made the decision to trust us, and way before the prospect has made the decision to buy.

That means we jumped ahead to **Step #4**: "Do I want it or not?" or jumped ahead to **Step #5**: "If I want it, okay, give me the details."

Too much. Too soon. And we skipped the most important question, "Can I trust you and what you are saying?"

Trust comes first.

Details come later.

But, how does our prospect make the decision to trust us?

This trust decision is instant. Ask yourself, "How long does it take me to make up my mind if I trust someone or not?"

In most cases, just a few seconds. Remember the old saying that first impressions are everything? There is a lot of truth in that.

People make up their minds about us instantly. Somehow they feel in the back of their minds that they can either trust us or not.

Imagine that we do a survey. We go out and ask one hundred people, "How do you make up your mind whether to trust someone or not?"

Their answer? "I don't know." But we press on. "You make lots of decisions, so how do you make up your mind?" They reply, "I don't know."

We don't stop. We pry even further. We ask, "So how do you know to trust someone or not?" They finally answer, "I just have a feeling."

So we ask, "Now, how do you get that feeling?" And of course they answer, "I don't know."

Prospects have no idea how they make up their minds!

Yet prospects make thousands of decisions every second as we learned earlier.

Here is the good news. We **do know** how prospects make up their minds. They make up their minds based upon automatic, stored programs that already exist in their minds.

Yes, stored programs. This is crucial for what we do first.

Why?

Because if we don't know how prospects make up their minds, we will make the following mistakes attempting to build trust and rapport. Here is how amateurs try to create trust and rapport:

#1. They are sincere.

#2. They are honest.

#3. They have integrity.

#4. They have their prospects' best interests at heart.

And none of these four things create trust and rapport!

Ouch.

Hard to believe? Well, let's look at some examples.

Case study #1:

Let's think back in time. Can we remember a time when we sat down with a prospect and the prospect didn't trust us or believe us? Yet, we were sincere, honest, had integrity, and we had that prospect's best interests at heart. Even though we had all four things, the prospect didn't trust us or believe us.

Case study #2:

Think of a con man. Is the con man sincere? Honest? Does he have integrity? Does he have his prospects' best interests at heart? Of course not. Yet the con man was able to create trust and belief in the first 15 seconds, and prospects willingly handed over their money.

The con man created trust and rapport without any of these four factors. Maybe the con man knows something we don't?

Yes, we can learn exactly what creates trust and rapport. And we don't have to use it for evil like a con man. We can use it to help our prospective clients get into action and fix their problems.

Please notice I am not saying to be insincere, be dishonest, have no integrity, or not have our prospect's best interest at heart. What I am saying is that these factors are not how most people make decisions to trust and believe us.

Mercedes-Benz, half-price.

Imagine I am a stranger. I come up to you and say, "I have Mercedes-Benz automobiles in the parking lot at half-price. Cash only. Want to buy one?"

What would you be thinking? Possibly you would be thinking, "The cars are stolen. There is something wrong with these cars. There has to be a catch. I don't know this person."

Now, Mercedes-Benz automobiles at half-price, well, that is a huge bargain. But because there is no trust and rapport, we will pass up even the best solution or the best bargain. No trust and no rapport means no business.

So even if we have the perfect solution for the client at an incredible discount, if that client does not trust us, he won't take that solution.

Step #2, "Can I trust you?" is the most important decision our prospect will make.

So, back to the original question. How do prospects make a decision to trust us and believe us?

Prospects use automatic, pre-existing, stored programs to decide to trust us and believe us.

Let's learn one program now.

Prospects have an automatic program: "I trust people who are more like me ... and tend to distrust people who are different from me."

If people are more like us, they will have the same viewpoint of the world. They will see things the same way. If they perceive that we both have the same viewpoint of the world, they can trust our conclusions.

That is why we tend to trust people of the same religion, the same ethnic background, people who like the same sports team, who are from the same city or country, who are members of the same political party, who like the same style of clothing, etc.

And, we tend to distrust people who have different viewpoints and beliefs. Our prospects want to know that we see the world the same way they do.

Here is an example. I am an American, I go to India. One billion Indian people around me. I meet another American. This American is more like me than the billion Indian people around me, so I feel instant rapport and trust with this stranger. I ask this stranger, "Where are you from?" He replies, "I am from Philadelphia." And then I say, "I am from San Francisco. We are neighbors!"

Well, we aren't neighbors. But we feel that we have a lot in common. There is instant trust and rapport.

Another example? Bernie is from England. He goes to America and visits Texas, the land of cowboys. With their deep southern accent, Bernie doesn't understand anyone. Finally, he meets another man from England who recommends a great fish 'n chip shop where they have silverware with the meal. Instant rapport! Bernie takes the recommendation without question, and enjoys a great British meal.

This is how quickly the decision is made by our prospects.

Another example? Imagine I come up to you and say, "Trust me, I am from the tax authorities and I am here to help you." You instantly think, "Tax authorities? You and I see things very differently. I think I will be skeptical. I won't trust you."

Yet one more example? As an American, when I speak to a group in England, I can say this: "Trust me, I am an American!"

Everyone laughs. They make an instant decision to be careful and skeptical, because Americans have very different viewpoints.

Do you see the world the same way I do?

This program tells our prospect whether to be open to us, or closed.

Do you remember Case Study #8 from the 13 case studies at the beginning of this book? The example was about a leader of a political party. If you are a member of that party, you naturally accept what the leader says as true. The leader has the same viewpoint as you. If you are a member of a different political party, then you will be skeptical and reject what the opposing leader says, because you have a different viewpoint.

So how do we let our potential clients know that we have similar viewpoints of his world?

We give them one or two facts that we both believe to be true. Now our prospects think, "Hey, you and I see the world the same way. I can trust what you say."

And that is all we ask.

We want our prospects to remove their sales alarm, their too-good-to-be-true filter, their "what's the catch" detector, their skepticism, their negativity and their resistance to new ideas. We want to remove all this mess, just so our prospects can be fair and hear a possible solution to their problems.

That's it.

When prospects have these negative programs running inside their heads, our message doesn't stand a chance. This isn't fair to our prospects. It is effectively withholding our solutions for their problems.

Our job is to open up our prospects' minds so they can hear our message. Our prospects can then decide if our message will enhance their lives or not.

It is all about getting trust and rapport - immediately.

We make our decision to trust or not to trust almost immediately. Stating common facts that we both believe early in our conversation helps build trust and open our prospect's mind.

Here are some examples of trust-building facts that might apply to a potential client. These statements won't work for every potential client, but they will give us an idea of how this trust-building works.

- "Life insurance can be expensive." (Prospect thinks, "Oh you are so right. You see the world like I do. You understand.")

- "Saving money for the future is almost impossible with prices going up and up." (Prospect thinks, "Finally, someone who understands how hard it is to save money.")

- "Nobody wants risky investments with their hard-earned savings." (Prospect thinks, "Read my mind. I couldn't sleep at night knowing my money could go down in value.")

- "It is impossible to read 1,800 new pages of tax regulations every year to maximize our retirement savings."

- "We want multiple options before we set a strategy."

- "Some people find financial advisors intimidating."

- "Most people think only rich people have a financial advisor."

- "Some people think they can't afford financial advice."

- "Most people are afraid of getting their financial advice on the Internet."

- "Smart people worry about their retirement."

What happens when our potential client hears one of these statements? He will set aside his fears, skepticism, and stress, because we think the same as he does. That's rapport.

Our prospect feels we will listen, understand, and help him resolve his problem. With this instant rapport, our potential client will be less likely to hold back and will give us a truer picture of his financial problem.

What happens when our potential client doesn't feel rapport in our initial interview?

The potential client is afraid to say, "I don't feel that you and I can work together. We just don't connect."

Instead, the potential client says:

- "I'll get back to you."

- "I need to think it over."

- "I have to talk it over with my partner."

- "I will be making a decision soon ..." And then he finds a competing financial advisor that he can "connect" with and feel secure.

So how important is a good opening fact or two?

Very important. We want to show our prospects that we understand their viewpoints. Notice how the word "most" in the following examples makes it easier for the prospect to agree:

- Most young families need insurance.

- Most insurance costs too much.

- Most parents don't have time to become investment experts.

- Most company retirement plans won't be enough.

- Most people want a financial counselor to help them with their finances.

- Most people want insurance in case of catastrophes and emergencies.

- Most people don't have extra money to invest.

- Most families want their investments to work hard for them.

- Most people want to feel secure.

- Most people would love to have their savings pay for their insurance.

- Most families need insurance, but their monthly budget is already tight.

- Most people want to make good investments and have healthy retirement plans.

"Most people?"

"Most" makes the factual statements easy. The word "most" triggers an automatic survival program in our prospect's mind. We survive by staying with the crowd. Being a loner is dangerous.

Want another word that has the same effect? Try "everybody" to start our statements.

When we say the word "everybody," here is what our prospect thinks:

"Am I part of nobody, or am I part of everybody? Well, if I am part of everybody, and everybody thinks this way, then I think that way too." It is one of those automatic programs we talked about earlier.

Some examples:

- Everybody knows that whole life insurance is the best value for this type of situation.

- Everybody says that term insurance is what young families need.

- Everybody knows young families need protection.

- Everybody knows insurance is the most efficient way to handle the estate tax problem.

- Everybody knows we eventually die.

- Everybody knows saving money is hard with family expenses.

- Everybody says insurance is too hard to understand.

- Everybody knows we don't want to overpay for our insurance.

Do our facts have to follow these formulas?

Of course not. These are just examples of facts. We can choose our own facts based upon the problem our client has. Want an example or two?

- "You are saving money already. You just need to decide if you want your savings to also protect your family."

- "We can give 20% of our income to taxes, or keep that tax money and invest it now."

- "Our government has a sophisticated plan to collect all the taxes it can from us. We need a strategy to keep more of our hard-earned money."

Bottom line.

Rapport, trust, and belief in us are the most important things we need to get from our prospects.

Are there other factors that will determine rapport? Of course. For example, maybe we ran over the prospect's dog the week before trying to get that appointment. That will definitely have an effect.

Or maybe they had a bad experience with a pushy salesperson and then created a strong sales resistance program. In that case, we will need better skills to overcome that program.

Think of rapport as being polite and having good manners. We wouldn't start a conversation with a friend by disagreeing with them. That is rude. And starting a conversation with people when we have an agenda? Well, people can smell that approach from miles away.

Rapport, trust and belief ... this is the biggest moment in our career.

What else can I do to build better trust and rapport?

Who do people like more? People who talk, or people who listen?

People love listeners. Why? Because nobody listens to them! Their family doesn't listen to them, their boss doesn't listen to them, even their friends and co-workers quickly lose interest in what they say.

Everyone thinks they are important. They feel what they say is important. Just with the simple act of listening, we can win our potential clients' favorable attention.

The penalty of not listening.

Imagine we owned an auto parts store. A customer walks in and says, "My car broke down. I need to buy a part."

We immediately jump in with our solution. "These spark plugs are the highest quality. They are tested, guaranteed, and a good value for the money. The manufacturer has over 100 years of experience in making the best spark plugs known to mankind. You should buy six spark plugs now."

Yes, we stopped listening. We jumped in with a solution way too quickly. Why is this wrong?

Because our customer did not need spark plugs! If we would have let the customer continue talking, the customer would have told us this: "My battery died. I need a new battery."

The penalty of not listening? Not only do we look stupid, but we will not be doing business with our potential clients. We can't possibly offer the correct solutions unless we know the problems.

Avoid talking too quickly.

We hear our prospect's problem. We have the solution. So, we want to start talking immediately about our solution.

Instead, let's take a few extra minutes to get the complete story of the problem. Vague problems are hard to solve. And, prospects hesitate to make decisions on vague problems. There is no urgency.

So what questions could we ask to investigate the prospect's problem even further? Here are a few.

- "Do you feel that this is the underlying problem?"

- "When did that problem occur?"

- "How long have you had this problem?"

- "How expensive will it be if we don't fix this problem?"

- "How soon do we need to fix this problem?"

The longer the prospect talks about his problem, the more vivid the problem becomes in his mind.

The longer the prospect talks and we listen, the deeper the rapport and trust will become.

When the pain is bad enough, prospects will close themselves.

Imagine that we receive a letter from our dentist. It says, "It is time for your annual checkup."

Do we panic? Do we immediately call our dentist? Do we ask for an appointment?

No. We are comfortable as we are. Dental prevention is not urgent. We will put off the appointment until a more convenient time.

But, then we get a toothache! Our toothache is unbearable. Our face is swollen on one side, we can only see out of one eye, we are sucking our meals through a straw, painkillers don't even dull the pain … this is serious.

We instantly call the dentist and insist on an appointment. The dentist replies, "I can get you an appointment on Monday at 10 AM, three weeks from today."

What do we say? Do we say, "Okay, thank you. I will wait for three weeks."

No!

Our pain is paralyzing. This is urgent. We tell the dentist, "I am coming in this morning. I will sit in your waiting room. If someone misses their appointment, I will be there to take their place. If no one misses their appointment, then during lunch when you're eating your sandwich, look inside my mouth!"

So when we are listening to prospects, allow enough time for the prospect to recognize the pain of not taking care of the problem. If the pain is bad enough, the prospect will seek out the solution with us immediately.

No further salesmanship or closing needed.

Repeat and intensify.

When we understand our prospect's problem, we should repeat the problem back to our prospect. This makes sure that there is no misunderstanding and that we both understand the problem clearly.

Now, we can intensify the urgency of solving that problem by the use of these words.

"Are you okay with ... ?"

Most people are not okay with keeping their problems. They want their problems solved. Let's see how using this phrase would sound in real life.

- "With today's inflation, are you okay with the negative return on your current savings account?"

- "Are you okay with not having the children's education insured?"

- "Are you okay with continuing to take these risks?"

- "Are you okay with the government taking those extra taxes on your retirement transfer?"

Of course we want to be cautious, and not be rude. So pick an appropriate and polite rephrasing of the prospect's problem. The phrase, "Are you okay with … ?" is very effective. But don't go too far.

Smile.

Want an easy way to build trust and rapport?

Smile.

This is one of those stored programs in our minds. We have this program almost from birth.

Imagine a baby lying in the crib. This baby is only a few months old. He can't roll over. He can't talk. He doesn't even understand language yet. But, the baby looks up at an adult, and how does the baby know which adult to trust?

The adult smiles. And even at a very early age, the baby can smile back.

So for years and years, we have had this program that smiling equals trust. Is this logical? No. Is it true that we can trust people who smile? Not always.

However, for most people, here is what happens. They see a person smile. They want to trust and believe what that person says.

That is just the way it is.

So to improve trust and rapport, let's remind ourselves to smile. We want the odds in our favor.

Yes, financial services are serious matters. But that doesn't mean we can't smile. It is important that we create that bond with prospects so they can hear the solutions we propose.

And finally ...

We already have rapport and trust with many of our prospects. In that case, we don't have to consciously take extra time on Step #2.

But, if we don't have rapport and trust, using these techniques can open our prospects' minds so that they can hear the good things we have to say.

Step #3: "Am I interested in what you say?"

Many new agents and advisors want to be solution-pushers. They want to push their solutions on prospects before the prospects have said they have a problem. That is selling people something they don't think they need, and that is hard.

Instead, we need to become problem-solvers. Prospects welcome problem-solvers. Instead of selling, we are advising them of an option that could solve their problem. Less stress. Less sales resistance. And, a lot more fun.

Now, prospects just won't walk up to us and say, "I have a problem." Most times we have to prompt them.

Not only do we have to prompt them, we have to be interesting. If we are not interesting, our prospect will change the subject. That means "no."

Let's look at some examples of prospects changing the subject.

Agent: "I have good life insurance that will last until age 100."

Prospect: "I just bought a new car. Would you like to ride in my new car?"

Agent: "We should talk about your retirement plan."

Prospect: "Did you see how many points the home team scored yesterday?"

Agent: "Are you concerned about your family's security?"

Prospect: "So how is the weather where you live? We almost flooded last night."

Changing the subject = "No."

People hate to say "no" to other people. It seems rude. Maybe the person lives next door. Maybe you have to see this person at work often. So, a more polite way of saying "no" to someone is to simply change the subject.

Other versions of people telling us "no" in a polite way? See if any of these sound familiar.

"I am busy right now."

"Let me get back to you."

"Let's talk about this later."

"I have other priorities I need to be focusing on now."

"Get back to me in a few weeks."

"Now is not the right time."

"Someone else handles that for me."

"Let me talk to my accountant and I'll get back to you."

The good news is that people are polite.

They are telling us "no" in an indirect way. They don't want to embarrass us.

Notice how quickly our prospects made this decision? In just seconds, our prospects can reject us. It is over.

Since we understand how prospects make fast decisions, we have to be careful about our first words. We have to capture our prospects' interest immediately.

There is no time to work up to the point. People are busy. They have more things to do with their time. People manage their time by quickly eliminating things they are not interested in. We don't want to be one of those things.

Then how do we start this conversation with our prospects?

With "ice breakers."

"Ice breaker" phrases to introduce our services.

Ice breakers are words or phrases that introduce a new subject into the conversation. At some point, we have to let our prospects know which services we have to offer. If we have been listening to our prospects' problems, we know which services will be interesting to them.

Let's look at some bad examples of ice breakers.

At a bar, a man wants to meet a lady.

He skips Step #1. (Who are you?)

He skips Step #2. (Can I trust you?)

Already we can see things are going badly. And then, he attempts to start his conversation with the lady by saying:

"Haven't I seen you somewhere before?"

Or,

"So what's your sign?"

Okay, these are terrible ice breakers. This man should brace for rejection. But all conversations have to start with an ice breaker.

We need to change our conversation from social chit-chat, or polite and pointless business talk, and get to work. We need to introduce our "interesting" service into the conversation.

Our ice breaker phrases may only be a sentence or two. At the end of these phrases, we realize that our prospect is going to make a final decision. Prospects are going to decide if we are interesting or not.

If we are not interesting, our prospects refuse to go further with the conversation. Time is valuable. The only way our prospects can conserve time is by eliminating conversations that are not interesting.

So, when we introduce our business into the conversation, what will we say? Good question.

Well, imagine that we listened to our prospect. The prospect told us that she has a large retirement fund payout coming shortly. She worries about taxes and where to reinvest the funds. Based upon this information, we might say this:

"Most people want a plan. They don't want to find out later that they missed the best options."

Let's put ourselves into our prospect's shoes. After this short, two-sentence ice breaker, she will make a decision. If she is not interested, she will change the subject. She might say, "I need to focus on my final days here at work. I will get to this problem later."

We take the hint. The answer is "no."

Or, in her mind, she could make the decision, "Yes! I need to know all the options. Please, when can we talk?"

Now, those are the words she is thinking. However, her internal "yes" decision will create this spoken reply to us:

"Oh really. What are some of the options?"

"That is interesting."

"I should take a look at some of these options."

"When can we talk?"

These answers represent a "yes" in her mind. She decided to do business with us.

If the answer was "no", she would not be asking additional questions. Nobody wants more information if their internal answer is "no." People who are not interested do not ask for additional information torture.

Closing?

Yes, this is when people begin their decision to do business with us … or not. This is especially true if we listen and know exactly which problems they want to solve.

People make decisions before we begin our presentations. Our presentations are facts we present to support our prospects' decisions.

Why does this work so well and so quickly?

Because we created strong rapport and trust in Step #2. That is why Step #2 is the most important thing we can do.

What are some examples of ice breakers that I can use?

Here are some formulas for phrases that will help. We have to get our message across in seconds. The following examples are only … examples. If we listen well, we will know which benefit to propose to solve our prospect's problem.

Formula #1.

"Most people."

Remember those words from earlier in this book?

Just by starting a conversation with "most people," we increase our chances of success. Why?

Because most people feel that they belong to the group called, "Most people." This is part of our survival program.

We survive because we don't take a lot of risks. We don't want to be the first person to eat a newly-discovered berry. We want other people to try that new berry first. We wait to see if others survive before we feel safe enough to eat that berry.

On Friday night, we go out to dinner. There are two restaurants side-by-side. The first restaurant is empty. The other restaurant is full of happy people toasting, drinking, singing, eating, and having a great time. Which restaurant are we going to choose for our dinner?

Well, most people would choose the crowded restaurant. They want to be with most people. The back of their minds say, "If more people were at the second restaurant, that means their food is better." Or, their mind might say, "I wonder if the first restaurant poisoned all of its customers? That is why no one is there."

Let's go to a large metropolitan city. Later that night, we have to walk through a dark, narrow alley. Do we want to walk through that alley alone? Or with a group of other people? With other people, of course. There is safety in numbers. That is why people follow the crowd. It is a good survival strategy.

"Most people" communicates survival to the stored decisions inside our prospects' minds. Two words. Done. This helps our ice breaker messages get accepted.

Remember the earlier example? As an ice breaker we said, "Most people want a plan. They don't want to find out later that they missed the best options."

This may be an appropriate ice breaker for that person.

More examples of using "most" or "most people" as an ice breaker?

- "Most private retirement funds have interesting tax-deferred options. Some of these options might be great for you."

- "Most people lose a lot of their retirement plan lump sum payment because they take the standard option. But thankfully, that can be avoided."

- "Most people hate watching the capital in their retirement fund get eaten by taxes. That is why their financial planner should help."

- "We work hard to build our retirement fund. Most retirees would like to see that fund continue to grow, instead of shrink from taxes."

So, will our prospects be interested?

If we say the right ice breaker, our chances are excellent.

Formula #2.

"I am just curious ... "

This innocent phrase is safe for the prospect, and rejection-free for us. Let's put this to work. Again, we will be talking to the lady who is concerned about her lump sum retirement.

"I am just curious, how many of the tax options have you explored?"

What will this lady think after this question? She might make the instant decision, "No. I am not interested."

Or, she will decide, "You seem to know many tax option solutions. Let's talk."

If she makes the crucial mental "yes" decision at this time, then we can move further into the details. But, the mental "yes" decision has to be made first.

Let's look at some more examples.

- "I am just curious, do you want to reduce your tax liability on this lump sum?"

- "I am just curious, have you read the latest tax deferral rulings?"

- "I am just curious, would it be okay if you looked at some of the options?"

- "I am just curious, should we look at some ways of conserving your capital?"

- "I am just curious, have you had a chance to research the dozens of re-investment options?"

- "I am just curious, are you thinking about taking an active or inactive role in managing your retirement fund investments?"

Easy conversation. No stress for the prospect or us.

But, Formula #3 is like putting our ice breaker on steroids. Let's see how Formula #3 not only creates interest, but also gets our prospects to make a decision if they want our service or not. All in seconds!

Formula #3.

"I've got a good story … "

Interesting? Guaranteed.

All we have to do is say the phrase, "I've got a good story … "

Remember those pre-stored programs in human minds? One of the programs is this. "If anyone, anywhere, at any time, starts telling a story, I have to listen to the story all the way to the end. I cannot go on in life until I know how the story ends."

Want to see this program in action?

We are walking to work. Ahead we see three co-workers. One of the co-workers is telling a story. What does our subconscious mind command us to do? It orders us, "You have to stop and listen to the story."

Stories are addictive. We can't resist stories.

Children from age two have this program. As soon as they can talk, they ask their parents, "Can you please tell me a story?"

We love stories. That is why we like books, movies, videos, Hollywood gossip, and more.

And as an added bonus, we remember stories. We can remember stories from age five. But, we can't remember a history date 15 minutes later for our examination. Our minds are optimized to remember stories. This means that when we tell a prospect a story, our prospect will remember our story. The story will constantly nag the inside of our prospect's brain when our story has a solution to his disturbing problem.

So, to get our prospect's interest, we tell our prospect a story.

How long should our story be?

Let's find out. We go out and survey 100 people. We ask this question, "Do you want to hear the long story or the short story?" What do you think the reply might be? Probably 100% of the people will tell us, "Please tell me the short story."

It is the same with our prospects. Remember, they are time-challenged. Too many things for them to do and think about. To conserve time, they make snap decisions to eliminate things they are not interested in.

How short should our story be? Some research shows that the human attention span averages eight seconds. Eight seconds? Yes.

We will have to capture our prospects' attention ... in just seconds. That means our initial story has to be short.

Here is the awesome bonus to short stories.

#1. We learned that people make decisions before the information.

#2. People make instant decisions. That means after a short 10- or 15-second story, they will make their "yes" or "no" decision to do business with us ... or not.

#3. If our prospect's decision is "no" after our short story, our prospect will change the subject. This "no" decision is final because the prospect will be moving on to another subject.

#4. If our prospect's decision is "yes" after our short story, that means our prospect made the mental "yes" decision to do business with us. We "closed" our prospect. Done. Now it is just a matter of some details to support our prospect's "yes" decision.

Amazing?

More than amazing!

We create a short story about how our service will solve our prospect's problem with a happy ending. This creates interest and closes our prospect at the same time. What a relief.

- No more endless trial closes.

- No more wondering what our prospect is thinking.

- No more stress.

- No more skepticism.

- No more long sales presentations and follow-up to prospects who will be telling us "no."

Think about the possibilities.

In just a few moments, we can handle Step #3 and Step #4 of our business. Remember those five steps? Here they are:

Step #1: "Who are you?"

Step #2: "Can I trust you?"

Step #3: "Am I interested in what you say?"

Step #4: "Do I want it or not?"

Step #5: "If I want it, okay, give me the details."

Is this the only way to talk to prospects? Of course not. But it is an awesome way. In just a few seconds, we can do the first four steps of our business.

The final step, the details, is a formality. It is fun to do the detailed presentation with prospects who already made the "yes" decision to do business with us.

Back to that story.

Our prospects want short stories. Their initial attention span is 10 or 15 seconds. We will adjust our stories to the services we offer, and to the problems of our target prospects.

Please note that our stories must comply with our country's laws and regulations. So please consider the following stories as only examples.

Here are some stories. At the end of each story, ask yourself this question: "What decision do I think my prospect will make at the end of this story?"

Also note that our prospect will not make a direct "yes" or "no" answer to our story.

The normal response for "no" is to change the subject by saying things like:

- "How is the weather where you live?"

- "Did you see that big sale announced this morning?"

- "Let me tell you about my kids."

- "So how long did it take you to get here today?"

These are all "no" answers. Let's respect that our prospect is not ready to do business with us now, may not need or want what we have to offer, or just hated our initial approach and offer.

Unfortunately, that is how quickly our prospects make decisions.

Our choices?

1. Move on to a qualified prospect.

2. Make a different initial offer.

How does "yes" sound?

The normal responses for "yes" are statements such as:

- "Tell me more."

- "How does that work?"

- "Is this safe?"

- "Are you sure?"

- "I have a question."

- "How much will this cost?"

Remember, prospects don't ask for additional information or want to extend the conversation if their answer is "no." All of the above questions and statements represent our prospects' way of saying "yes" to doing business with us.

Finally, some sample stories.

"I've got a good story." The prospect replies, "What is the story?"

We say, "My client in Middletown used to worry every night. His entire pension was 100% invested in his company's stock. He couldn't sleep. We diversified 40% of his pension into a growth mutual fund. Now he sleeps a lot better."

How would you expect the prospect to reply? Maybe the reply would sound like this:

- "Tell me more about this client of yours from Middletown."

- "I should probably diversify also."

- "My pension plan is locked right now, but I will have some options in January."

- "I worry about that also."

The above "yes" decisions were easy to recognize.

How about another story?

"Most teachers here in the school district have a good pension plan. However, many of the teachers have young families. Their biggest concern is not about retirement, but if they have enough insurance to guarantee their children's future education. They now combine their insurance and savings so they can stay within their family budget."

If our prospect had a young family, what would be the natural choice? Their "yes" answers might sound like this:

- "How did they do that?"

- "That is interesting. What did they do?"

- "Yes, keeping within a budget is hard with small children."

- "Insurance is expensive. Would this cost a lot?"

- "I have trouble saving money now. How does this work?"

How about another story?

"My grandfather was smart. He wanted 100% of his estate to go to his grandchildren. Instead of giving one third of his entire life's savings to the government in taxes, he invested a little bit in life insurance to cover his entire estate tax. I appreciated that. I figured he knew that I could use the money more than the government."

Notice what is happening?

With this simple story technique, we are combining:

Step #3: "Am I interested in what you say?"

Step #4: "Do I want it or not?"

We don't have to "close" our prospects. They do it themselves. Their answers tell us if they have made a "yes" decision or if they are not interested. No ridiculous high-pressure salesman closes.

This takes a huge burden off our shoulders. In the beginning of our careers, we believe closing our prospects will be difficult. We plan, plot, and overthink the situation. People just make ... decisions ... naturally.

As a more skilled professional, we understand that decisions are immediate. Decisions occur before we even begin our presentation. Things don't get much easier than this.

Now, you might be thinking, "If my prospects make their decisions before my presentation, then what do I say to finish my presentation? I don't want to go on talking and talking and hope they volunteer to move forward."

Yes, we might need a few simple closes to prompt them to stop our conversation and to move forward. We will get to them shortly.

But for now, let's celebrate the ease of getting our prospects to make decisions to do business with us. This is all under the radar, where the prospects don't notice. They don't understand how they make decisions or when. But, we do. Life is good.

A word about stories.

Stories are our best way to communicate with our potential clients. As humans, we think in stories. We dream in stories. We understand the world in stories.

Think of it this way. The best storytellers win. To accelerate our business, we should build a huge catalog of appropriate stories for our potential clients.

We will use these stories to meet people, to create trust, to create interest, to close, to overcome objections, and to eliminate skepticism. Sometimes we just need a clear story so that the prospect can see the big picture. Here is an example of a story that does this.

"Why do I need a financial advisor?"

Imagine our prospect wants to plan his financial future on his own. He reads a few articles on the Internet. He receives some random advice from strangers. Now he feels that he can bypass the services his financial advisor offers. Well, arguing with our potential client will only ruin our trust and rapport. The better strategy would be to tell a story. Here is an example of a story we can use.

"Imagine you and I approach a minefield that we have to cross. One small mistake could be fatal. Do we want to risk crossing that minefield by trial and error? Do we want to cross that minefield ourselves? Or, would we feel better if we could follow someone who has crossed that minefield many times before?

"Financial planning and tax planning are similar. Because of the countless laws, regulations, and tax rulings, we don't want to make amateur mistakes that might cost us dearly. That is why we use financial advisors. Financial advisors cross that minefield every day for hundreds of clients. We can help you with planning around laws and regulations that are not apparent to the general population. We want safe approaches with our hard-earned savings."

What do you think our prospect's decision will be after this story?

This easy story helps our prospect understand the dangers of planning with limited knowledge and resources.

Step #4:
"Do I want it or not?"

Not much to discuss here.

If we use "ice breakers" or short stories, then our prospects can decide if they want our services or not.

"Closing" is nothing more than getting our prospect's decision. If our prospect's decision is "yes" to our product or service, we move on to Step #5, our presentation.

There is no need for a presentation to a prospect who makes a "no" decision. That is a relief. There is nothing worse than giving a presentation to a prospect who is leaning back, folding his arms, and impatiently waiting for us to finish.

The "no" decision is obvious. We irritate the prospect and waste our time.

Think of Step #4 this way.

A. Our prospect has a problem.

B. Our prospect trusts us (Step #2).

C. Our prospect wants to fix his problem now, or not.

D. The decision is made.

If the prospect wants to fix his problem now, then, and only then, will we give a presentation with the details of how we will fix his problem.

Is Step #4 important?

Of course. Our job is to get "yes" decisions from our prospective clients. Ultimately, this is what we get paid for.

But Step #4, getting our prospect's decision, is easy. We did the hard work in Step #2 (creating trust and rapport) and in Step #3 (getting our prospect's interest).

We accomplish these steps in a relaxed, short conversation. We don't have to waste our time with fruitless or frustrating discussions.

So let's move forward.

Step #5:
The presentation
and details.

Our prospective client wants a solution to his problem. We have it. Now is the time to make our potential client feel secure by describing our solution in detail.

How much detail?

That depends on our prospective client.

- Extremely analytical prospects may want pages of charts and graphs.

- Other potential clients feel relieved that we will handle the details so that they can go about their other business. They are comfortable with letting a professional sort things out for them.

This should be the easiest part of our client engagement. The "yes" decision has been made. Our potential client is sitting on our side of the table as a partner, instead of as an adversary. We are looking at the solution together. No convincing or manipulation needed.

Let's take a look at a few styles of presentations.

We will first start with a minimal presentation for a potential client who wants little detail. This type of client wants to invest his time in his business and life, instead of investing hours poring over the micro-details of our solution.

Please note: In all of these presentation examples, we will leave out the required disclaimers and disclosures required by your country or regulatory bodies. Obviously these will vary from country to country, and from product to product. As licensed professionals, we should already have proficiency in this area.

Minimal presentation.

This minimal presentation is for potential clients who have more important things to focus on in their lives.

We could start off our presentation by saying this:

"I can give you a two-hour review of each and every detail, a 20-minute presentation, or a two-minute summary. Which would you prefer?"

Most of our potential clients will say, "Just give me the two-minute summary."

When we have trust and rapport with our client, the presentation is simple. They realize that we know a lot more about financial planning than they do. They have chosen to do business with us, and they want us to handle the research and details.

Will every potential client ask for the two-minute summary? Of course not. A small percentage of potential clients have extremely analytical personalities. They will want to know ... everything!

Our mission is to help our clients in the way they want to be helped. Most clients want little or no information, while others may want to discuss details for hours until they feel secure.

Short presentations are okay.

Our potential client makes a decision to do business with us long before our presentation starts. We don't even consider a presentation until we have:

- Built rapport.
- Gotten the trust of our potential client.
- Created interest in our offering.
- Helped our potential client to make a "yes" decision.

Clients must first decide if they want to take care of their problem ... now.

For those clients that want a short presentation, let's be polite. Before we start our monologue of facts, we should consider their feelings.

Who should decide what they want to know? Should we force them to hear everything we think they should know? Or, will we be more polite and talk to them about what they want to know?

The answer is obvious.

So, how are we going to know what our potential client wants to know? That is easy. We ask. We don't guess. And by asking, our potential client will tell us exactly what he wants to know. Here is the initial question we will ask.

"What would you like to know first?"

Magically, our potential client will tell us exactly what he wants to know first. Can't get more accurate than that. This is good service.

But here is the real reason we should start with the question, "What would you like to know first?"

When potential clients ask for presentations, some may still feel some sales resistance. We have seen negative clients sit back, fold their arms, and set up a wall of their mental defenses. This question disables those negative actions. Simply say, "What would you like to know first?"

Want to remove all sales tension instantly? Just say those words.

What does the potential client think after hearing this question? He thinks, "This person isn't a salesman. He is going to let me talk. I won't have to listen to some stupid monologue. Let me tell him exactly what I want to know first."

And at this moment, he releases his sales tension.

What happens next?

We will answer this question as quickly as humanly possible, but still answer it completely. The shorter our answer, the better. We don't want to use this opportunity to pour on more sales benefits.

Why a short answer?

Because additional information will create new threads of indecision. We don't want to overwhelm our potential client with too many options and features to think about.

Here is an example. We ask, "What would you like to know first?"

The prospect replies, "What is the name of the life insurance company?"

We answer, "The Wonderful Life Insurance Company."

That is the correct answer. Short and to the point.

Here is an example of the incorrect answer.

The prospect asks, "What is the name of the life insurance company?"

We answer, "The Wonderful Life Insurance Company. It is a five-star rated company. With over 20 billion real estate assets, it is one of the leading companies in our area."

Now, what might our prospect be thinking?

He might be thinking, "Five-star rated company? Maybe that isn't good? Should I be going with a six-star or a seven-star rated company? And real estate! Real estate is risky. Interest rates are too high now. I don't want to lose my money to real estate investing. Our local area is in a recession. This can't be good."

See what happens?

We introduced additional threads of information that will create doubt and confusion in our prospect's mind. Let's be polite. Let's just answer what our prospect wants to know.

So after quickly answering the first question, we will say this to our potential client:

"What would you like to know next?"

We will continue by asking the question, "What would you like to know next?"

Why?

Because each potential client has different interests and different concerns. We are customizing our presentation to address his needs.

And we will continue asking the question, "What would you like to know next?" until our prospect runs out of questions!

For some prospects, one question will be all they have. Others, well, it could go on for a long time. But the extra time is the prospect's choice, not ours.

So what do we say when our prospect runs out of questions?

STEP #5: THE PRESENTATION AND DETAILS.

"What would you like to do next?"

This is one of the most respectful closing questions anyone could ask. Our prospects won't feel pressured. We have their best interests at heart. We are asking what **they** would like to do next.

Well, what do you think our prospect might want to do next? Here are some possible answers we might hear to this closing question.

- "Let's get started."

- "Can I pay this monthly instead of annually?"

- "What do I have to do next to move this money from my current pension plan?"

- "Should I let my tax advisor know that I will be investing in a tax-deferred plan?"

- "Can we fill out the paperwork on Friday? I have more time then."

- "Let's meet on Tuesday to finalize the paperwork. This will give me more time to get my records together."

All of the above are "yes" decisions. Easy and stress-free.

But what would a "no" decision sound like? Here is an example.

Prospect: "I need to think it over."

Financial advisor: "Until when?"

Prospect: "Until the holidays."

Financial advisor: "Which holidays?"

Prospect: "Christmas 2047."

Financial advisor: "Should I call you then, or will you call me?"

Prospect: "I will call you."

That "no" decision was easy to identify. Want another example?

The prospect says, "This is too much information. I can't make up my mind. My father died broke, my grandfather died broke, and I want to die broke just like them. I feel like jumping off a cliff. Would you help me with a push? And paying more taxes makes me feel like a professional victim. I like it when people feel sorry for me. I wasn't loved as a child."

Well, maybe our prospect is not this dramatic, but we understand "no" decisions when we hear them.

Let's review.

We have our prospect's trust.

Our prospect made a mental "yes" decision before our presentation began.

We supplied the facts that our prospect needed to feel good about his decision.

We used a simple conversation to deliver the facts instead of an inflexible sales presentation filled with too much information.

Want another example of a short presentation?

Now remember, the potential client made the mental decision to do business with us earlier. We don't have to use our presentation as a sales tool to convince our potential client to do business with us. Our presentation is simply delivering enough facts and data to satisfy prospects that they made a good decision.

Let's try this opening sentence to introduce our short presentation:

"So here is the short story."

That's it. People love the short story version of anything! We have busy lives and our brains are already overloaded. "Short story" sounds great! And we know that a short story is enough for most prospects to make their final decision.

Let's review. We finished our first four steps.

Step #1: "Who are you?"

Step #2: "Can I trust you?"

Step #3: "Am I interested in what you say?"

Step #4: "Do I want it or not?"

And now, it is time for:

Step #5: "Yeah, I want it, so give me the details."

The first words of Step #5 can be, "So here is the short story."

So let's look at a few examples of using these opening presentation words.

- "So here is the short story. You worry about paying a huge tax bill when you take your lump sum retirement. Our company specializes in preparing the correct paperwork to make your transfer easy and tax-deferred so your retirement money will keep working for you. What else would you like me to describe or cover with you?"

- "So here is the short story. You worry that if you get sick or die, what will your spouse and children do for money? This combination insurance policy guarantees they are cared for and you won't have to worry. Are there any other details you would like me to discuss?"

- "So here is the short story. You don't want to retire broke like your father. You told me the consequences. Investing this small amount monthly assures you of a better retirement. Anything else we should talk about?"

- "So here is the short story. You are the brightest engineer at your firm. But, you don't have time to study to become a professional investor. You want professional investment advice. We can take care of that for you. Anything else we should cover?"

In the above examples, we added a question at the end to avoid that dreadful "dead silence." This question gently allows the potential client to say, "Okay, let's get started on this."

And, if there are more details needed, the potential client feels comfortable asking now.

The secret to this rejection-free approach is that the "close" or "decision" happened earlier at Step #4. We are just filling in some details with our presentation.

But sometimes I need a longer, more formal presentation.

Let's learn another way of presenting in the following chapter. Not one presentation style will fit every client in every situation.

Ready?

15 magic words.

Imagine that last week we conducted a fact-finding interview with our potential client. The client described his financial status. He asked us to research and propose a solution.

On our follow-up appointment, our potential client expects a full report.

Getting started.

The first order of business is to move the conversation away from social chit-chat and coffee, and get down to business. An easy way to do that is with this phrase, "So John, from my understanding, we have 45 minutes to discuss how we can help you get the insurance coverage you need, at an affordable price, and get your retirement savings program started without breaking the budget. Is that about right?"

Notice how we have given three distinct benefits. This gives value to the prospective client. At least one of the benefits will be of extreme interest to him. If we use only one benefit, we may miss the mark. As professionals, we should have a list of specific benefits that we can offer. Then, it will only be a matter of choosing three benefits that target our potential clients' needs. Here is a partial list of benefits to get our ideas flowing:

- Save money on taxes.

- Insure the family.

- Pay off the mortgage in case of premature death.

- Guarantee our children's education.

- Protect our income in case of accident or sickness.

- Retire early.

- Save money for retirement within our current budget.

- Maximize our estate.

- Increase our return with tax-deferred investments.

- Achieve capital growth instead of the low return from savings.

After mentioning our three benefits, we will finish our opening by saying, "Is that about right?"

Then we pause.

We wait.

Now is the time for our potential client to commit to the process. Without this commitment, we will struggle. We must have him "buy into" wanting to proceed now.

Showtime!

Now that we have our prospect's agreement, we can begin our presentation. Rather than a friendly conversation, our prospect is expecting a formal proposal. We should meet our prospect's expectations.

A more structured presentation will use the "15 magic words" format. This is an excellent way to make formal proposals and to get final agreement from potential clients.

Here are some benefits of using this more structured approach:

- Increase our conversions.

- Make sure our potential client can afford the solution.

- Look more professional.

- Keep the presentation on track and moving forward.

- Allow the prospect to feel in control.

- Help bring the presentation to a smoother conclusion.

- Respect our potential client's time.

The magic happens with the initial words. These words will help the prospect to be open-minded as we go through our checklist presentation describing the solution to his problem.

We sit down with the prospect. This is our chance to set the pace of our meeting. Here are the basic 15 words:

"Here is our agenda. Is there anything you wish to add, or is this okay?"

Then we immediately pass a copy of our agenda/solution to our potential client. The top page can be a simple checklist that we will follow in our structured presentation.

We make the checklist.

We determine the order of the conversation.

What is our prospect thinking? Our prospect is probably thinking, "Wow. This person is organized. This professional took the time to personally investigate and work on a solution for me. Very considerate. I appreciate that this is organized and won't take much time."

Let's break down these 15 magic words.

"Here is our agenda."

This signals professionalism. And, this lets the prospect know that this meeting is not going to go on forever.

"Is there anything you wish to add?"

This statement makes the prospect feel that he is in control. If we missed a problem in our initial interview, here is a chance for our prospect to add it to this agenda. Asking our prospect for any additions signals that this is a two-way conversation. This is not an impersonal monologue sales presentation.

The prospect has to review the problems we stated in order to see if anything is missing. This review reinforces to the prospect that he has problems that he wants to solve. On our checklist, we will leave a line or two empty to write in any additional problems that need to be discussed.

"Or is this okay?"

Again, we pause.

And wait.

Our prospect will then agree. That is our signal that our prospect is ready to move forward with a solution to his problems.

The checklist.

We may have a checklist for the initial fact-finding interview. The basic information we put on this checklist will depend on our products and services.

In some cases we will only need simple facts such as date of birth, income, and problems to be solved. In other cases, we may need more detailed facts such as tax implications, accountant's name, the type of estate assets and more.

The good news is that we create the checklist. This gives us control of the conversation and control of the solutions.

In the following example, we will make a sample checklist for someone who wants to move his pension because of early retirement. Remember, we create the checklist. Be flexible. The checklist is to serve us and our potential client.

At the top.

Our potential client will look here first. This is a great place to put our client's name. This shows that it is not some generic checklist we are using. It shows the client we have invested time and energy into his situation and possible solutions.

A good thing to add is the amount of time expected to cover this agenda. For example, if you scheduled your follow-up appointment for 40 minutes, put 40 minutes in the top right-hand corner. This will make the client more relaxed because he will see a finite time limit. If you want to be more impressive, make the amount of time in the upper right-hand corner less than the appointment time. For example, if the appointment is for 40 minutes, place 30 minutes in the top right-hand corner. Prospects will feel instant relief.

What is next?

Restate the problems the potential client wants to solve.

This gives us a chance to remind our potential client of the pain of keeping his problems. If his problems are not causing any pain or discomfort, there would be little or no incentive to look for solutions.

Further down our checklist, we can list some benefits of solving our potential clients' problems. These benefits could include everything from peace of mind to estate tax savings.

Here is our chance to insert possible solutions to our potential clients' problems. This is where we put in the features and benefits of our solutions.

For example, a small monthly premium would provide insurance that no matter what happens, the children would have money for university. Or, starting a personal pension would supplement the inadequate pension benefits from work.

Next, a discussion about costs.

Few solutions are free. Our potential clients expect that. Costs could include the monthly premium. Or, how much money someone would invest monthly in their private pension plan. Or our advisor fees. Nobody expects free professional advice.

And finally, a recap of the expected benefits. We need to remind our potential client that the costs will yield the benefits he wants.

And that's it.

This is a simple outline of a sample checklist. Our checklist is nothing more than a sheet of paper. We place this paper on top of the folder that has all the facts, figures, graphs, documents, reports and solutions.

Why do we do this on one page?

"A confused mind always says 'no.'"

Our prospective clients employ us as advisors to simplify complicated financial problems. They don't want to make individual assessments and decisions on a multitude of conflicting factors. What they want us to do is streamline the process and summarize it neatly. They are not employing us to make it more difficult.

So instead of hundreds of possibilities and solutions, we can narrow down their decisions to this simple one-page checklist.

As we go through this checklist, we should seek some sort of agreement on every item. For example, when we talk about the problems, we could ask, "These seem to be the problems we discussed earlier, right?"

Or when we talk about the cost, we could say, "And this

figure is within the budget we talked about earlier, right?"

We shouldn't move forward through our checklist until we have agreement on each point. We don't want our prospect at the end of our presentation to be thinking, "Oh my. Now I have six or eight different things to think about." Instead, we want to bring these complicated financial matters down to a simple choice.

The prospect's choice?

"Will this solution solve my problem?"

We make the choice easy for our potential client.

At the end of our checklist review, our prospect can make the decision to move forward. If we are looking for a way to close the conversation, so we don't continue with endless chitchat, let's move on to an easy question that gets decisions.

Finishing and getting a decision.

It is the end of the presentation. Our prospective client looks at us. We look at him. No one is talking. Seems a bit uncomfortable. So who should make the first move?

Well, we can stare at each other forever, and most prospects will sit there until we talk. So what should we say?

Now, we know the decision to do business with us happened early in our interaction with our prospective client. If the prospective client didn't want to do business with us, we wouldn't even be giving a presentation. But many times there seems to be this little uncomfortable situation at the very end.

We don't want to be the first one to talk because we are afraid of rejection. Or, we don't want to appear pushy to the prospective client.

The prospective client is programmed to delay decisions as long as humanly possible. That is why this uncomfortable situation exists.

Taking control.

It is up to us to take control, get an immediate decision, and move on to finish the final paperwork. How are we going to do this?

Easy.

We will use a simple nine-word phrase. This nine-word phrase will accomplish the following:

1. Ask for the final decision rejection-free.

2. Show the prospective client that we have his best interests at heart.

3. Relax the prospective client by giving him choices.

4. Ask the prospective client to make an immediate choice.

5. And finally, take advantage of the stored programs we have that compel us to take the easiest choices, not the hardest choices.

We can do all this with only nine words?

Of course. We just have to use the correct nine words.

So at the end of our presentation, when that dead silence occurs, we will say the following nine words:

"So what is going to be easier for you?"

These nine words communicate the following to our prospective client:

1. We are asking for a decision in a rejection-free manner.

2. Show the prospective client that we have his best interests at heart. We want to know what is going to be easier for him.

3. Our nine words offer our prospective client choices. He now feels relaxed because we are not forcing a single solution on him.

4. Our nine-word question asked the prospective client to make a choice. When he makes the choice, there is no more "thinking it over." This helps remove procrastination.

5. And finally, we are all programmed this way. We want to do what is easier for us, not what is harder for us. So when the prospective client takes the easier solution, the decision is final. No more closing or selling needed on our part.

What kind of choices should we give our prospective client?

Having two choices makes it easier for decisions. The more complicated the choices, the harder it is for a prospective client to make a decision. There would just be too much to think about in such a short time.

We all know the old saying: "A confused mind always says 'no.'"

What are the two choices we should give our prospective client?

Choice #1: Do nothing. Keep his circumstances the same. Keep his unsolved problems. Continue on in life with the exact same painful situation he has been living in. No changes. No improvement in his financial situation.

Choice #2: Move forward now and solve his problems. Take our advice, do business with us, and move forward with an improved situation in his life.

Simple, right?

We condense a multitude of factors and choices and boil them down to a simple decision.

There is no in-between. There is no delaying. There is only keeping the situation as it is, or improving it.

For the prospective client, two choices. No pressure. Just pick the choice that is easier for him.

This is a win-win for everyone. The prospective client can choose to keep his life the same, or to improve his life with our solutions. And for us, we walk away with the decision to move forward ... or not. And, it is all finished politely and without rejection.

So let's take a look at some examples of how we could phrase these choices.

How does this nine-word statement sound in real life?

Choice #1: We describe keeping the current situation.

Choice #2: We describe what happens when the potential client implements our solution.

Here are some examples.

"So what is going to be easier for you? To receive your retirement pension now in one lump sum, and pay a huge tax bill from your settlement? Or, to transfer your money to this tax-deferred pension plan so that you can keep 100% of your capital invested?"

"So what is going to be easier for you? To save for your children's education and hope that nothing happens along the way? Or to save for your children's education with this insurance plan, and be guaranteed that they will have money for university no matter what happens?"

"So what is going to be easier for you? To continue worrying about the big mortgage you have, and who will pay it if you cannot? Or, to activate this inexpensive insurance policy to guarantee that your family will always have a place to live?"

"So what is going to be easier for you? To take classes, search the Internet, and learn financial investing, while taking that time away from your business? Or to use the financial advice from our trusted financial experts?"

Simple.

Polite.

Respectful.

Why prospects say, "I want to think it over."

"I want to think it over."

"I need to check with my spouse."

"I should run this by the board of directors first."

"Let me sleep on this."

We hate it when our prospects delay their decision. But, this excuse happens over and over again. Why?

Because it is **normal** for humans to delay decisions as long as possible.

Normal? Yes.

Let's see how humans got this program to delay decisions.

First, think back in time. Have we ever made a bad decision? Of course. Now, how did we feel about that bad decision? We felt bad.

Later, we thought about that decision again. Then, we felt bad … again. We do this over and over. Bad decisions are hard to forget.

So what happens in our mind? Our subconscious mind thinks we repeated that bad decision hundreds or even thousands of times. How does our subconscious mind react?

It forms a program that says, "Don't make any more decisions. Delay decisions as long as possible. We don't want the trauma and drama of another bad decision."

So the objection, "I want to think it over," is completely normal when talking to humans. We programmed our minds to avoid decisions at all costs.

It gets worse.

Other people program our minds to avoid decisions also. Think about jobs. Have you ever heard this from a boss? "Please make your own decisions on what to do. There is no need to follow our company policies and instructions."

That has never happened. Employers insist that the employees follow instructions precisely. There is no reward for making independent decisions. However, there are severe penalties for making independent decisions. Yes, if we had a job, we were programmed to never make decisions.

Now that we understand that delaying decisions is normal, we won't be surprised when we get that objection. We won't panic. Instead, let's learn how to handle that objection professionally.

The basic rules of objections.

There is no communication unless there is agreement.

If we disagree with our prospects' objection, communication stops. Here is why.

1. Do prospects trust and like people who disagree with them? No. When we disagree, we harm our rapport and trust. This creates a huge problem. This

is the first reason we must agree instead of disagree with our prospects' objections.

2. The human mind can only entertain one thought at a time. So imagine we are listing all the reasons why our prospect is wrong. What is our prospect thinking while we argue with his objection? The prospect is not thinking about what we are saying. In fact, the prospect isn't even listening to what we are saying. Instead, the prospect is collecting reasons in his mind to support his position when we shut up.

Now our situation is this.

Our prospect is not listening to us. Our prospect is thinking of more reasons to lay out as soon as we stop talking. This is a lose-lose proposition.

So how do we handle this dilemma?

First, we must agree with our prospect. This is not hard to do. All we have to do is try to look at things from our prospect's point of view. We don't know what happened to our prospect prior to our conversation. We don't know the background of our prospect. We don't know what drama or trauma has happened in our prospect's life that creates this objection. Just having a little empathy for our prospect makes it easy to agree with their objection.

So here are the first words that we will say to our prospect after the objection, "I want to think it over." We will say this:

"Relax. It is okay."

When we open with, "Relax ... " How does our prospect feel?

Our prospect lets out a deep sigh of relief. Our prospect releases the tension of having to defend his objection. We keep that trust and rapport we worked so hard to get. It is almost impossible to sell to a scared prospect.

Then, we add the phrase, "It is okay." The prospect relaxes further. We signaled to the prospect that we respect any decision that he makes.

Let's review.

1. Our prospect relaxes.

2. He likes us because we listen.

3. We continue having rapport and trust.

4. Our prospect is now ready to hear the words we want to say.

Stop fighting our prospect's programs.

We are not going to change the prospect's program to delay and avoid making decisions.

That task is huge, and we don't have much time. It takes time to remove long-held programs.

Instead, here is our strategy. We will point out to the prospect that:

"Not making a decision ... is making a decision not to do it."

That's right. When we delay a decision, we are making a decision to keep our circumstances the same.

Here are a few examples.

Example #1. We are standing in the airport waiting for our airplane to board. They announce, "Final boarding." Now, if we want to wait and think it over for 15 minutes, what happens? Our plane leaves without us. Not making a decision to board immediately was making a decision to stay where we are. Not making a decision was a decision to stay in the airport.

Example #2. We are standing in the middle of a busy expressway. Cars and trucks are rapidly approaching us. We think to ourselves, "Do I run to the right, or do I run to the left?" But we decide to think about it for a while. What happens? Smash! A car hits us. By delaying and not making a decision to move either right or left, we effectively made a decision to stand as human target practice for speeding traffic.

Example #3. Our retirement savings are zero. We worry about our future. But where and how do we start? Should we set aside a percentage of our income? Should we wait to see if we get an end-of-the-year bonus? Should we hope to get an inheritance from an unknown rich relative?

So we think and think and think. Not making a decision to start saving now means the days, weeks, months and years will continue to go by. Now it will be even harder and more expensive to save for retirement. Not making a decision to start now is a decision to have no savings plan for our retirement.

A decision to delay and think it over is ... a decision to keep our current situation.

So we say to our prospect, "Relax. It is okay ... " Now here is what we are going to do next. We will point out to our prospect that he can't hide from a decision. We will let our prospect know that not making an immediate decision ... is a decision to keep his circumstances the same.

We are removing the luxury and safe feeling of putting off a decision until later.

Now the prospect must make a decision. We will explain that delaying a decision to work with us is making a decision to keep his same situation. So let's point out that situation now. Here are some examples:

- "Relax. It is okay to make a decision to leave your family uninsured today."

- "Relax, it is okay to make a decision to keep your money in a negative yield savings account today, and continue losing money every hour."

- "Relax, it is okay to keep your entire life's retirement in your company stock, and continue to worry every night if your company's stock will go up or down."

- "Relax, it is okay to give 30% of your estate to the government instead of moving your estate to a tax-favored investment for your grandchildren."

So instead of fighting with the prospect, let's agree with our prospect. Then tell our prospect, "Relax. It is okay to make a decision to stay where you are."

Let's ask ourselves, "How does my prospect feel now?" Our prospects should feel respected, heard, and we can continue our conversation cordially.

But, it gets better.

Consequences.

All decisions have consequences.

Out of fairness to our prospect, we should point out the consequences of the decision to stay where he is. Here is our chance to remind our prospect of the original problem he wanted to solve. At this point, depending on our relationship with our prospect, we can lightly mention the consequences. Or if we choose, we can powerfully point out the huge consequences of not making the decision to move forward.

Let's take the original examples and enhance the consequences.

- "Relax. It is okay to make a decision to leave your family uninsured today. I know the stress of worrying about the family that you love makes it difficult to sleep at night. You want the very best for your family."

- "Relax, it is okay to make a decision to keep your money in a negative yield savings account today, and continue losing money every hour. Because of inflation, you are losing $81 every day your bank holds your money hostage in your savings account."

- "Relax, it is okay to keep your entire life's retirement in your company stock, and continue to worry every night if your company's stock will go up or down. I know you worry that a single decision by the HR department, or the Board of Directors, could wipe out your entire life's work for your retirement. You and I never know when a company might accept an attractive buyout offer."

- "Relax, it is okay to give 30% of your estate to the government instead of moving your estate to a tax-favored investment for your grandchildren. In your case, you will be donating $436,000 to the government instead of giving it to your grandchildren."

Okay. Our prospect now knows the consequences of making a decision not to do business with us at this time.

But this gets even better.

Now we have open communication with our prospect. This gives us another opportunity to review the benefits of doing business with us. At this point, we will point out the benefits of making a decision to move forward.

Our conversation will now sound like this:

- "Relax. It is okay to make a decision to leave your family uninsured today. I know the stress of worrying about the family that you love makes it difficult to sleep at night. You want the very best for your family. But, it is also okay to make a decision to insure your family tonight. Now you can have the protection you wanted, and remove that stress from your mind. Your family will feel secure about the future, and the children's future education."

- "Relax, it is okay to make a decision to keep your money in a negative yield savings account today, and continue losing money every hour. Because of inflation, you are losing $81 every day your bank holds your money hostage in your savings account. But, it is also okay to make a decision to move part of your savings account to a capital growth fund. Now you have a chance to make inflation work for you. This means the money you save now can have value when you retire. You won't have to idly sit by and watch your money decrease in value as inflation grows and grows."

- "Relax, it is okay to keep your entire life's retirement in your company stock, and continue to worry every night if your company's stock will go up or down. I know you worry that a single decision by the HR department, or the Board of Directors, could wipe out your entire life's work for your retirement. You and I never know when a company might accept an attractive buyout offer. But, it is also okay to make a decision to diversify part of your retirement plan. It is okay to stop risking your entire retirement plan on one roll of the dice. Now you can be sure that you will always have something for your retirement."

- "Relax, it is okay to give 30% of your estate to the government instead of moving your estate to a tax-favored investment for your grandchildren. In your case, you will be donating $436,000 to the government instead of giving it to your grandchildren. But, it is also okay to make a decision to invest in this tax-favored investment that will preserve more of your estate for your grandchildren. I am sure your grandchildren will appreciate the money much more than the government."

Let's review this technique.

#1. Agree with our prospect's objection. If we argue, our prospect won't be listening to us anyway. Instead, we will say, "Relax. It is okay."

#2. Remove the luxury of procrastination from our prospect's mind. Let the prospect know that he is making a decision to keep his situation the same.

#3. Point out the consequences of making a decision to keep circumstances the same.

#4. Point out the benefits of making the decision to act now. Tell the prospect, "But, it is also okay to make a decision to take action now." This reminds the prospect that he has to make a decision now.

That's it. In a polite and civil way, we let the prospect know that there is no "thinking it over." Our prospect understands they have to make a decision now.

And that is it?

Yes.

Most objections disappear when we realize that prospects make decisions early in our conversations.

Presentations are easier when our prospects make "yes" decisions before we start describing our solutions.

When we change how and when we get decisions, everything changes in how prospects react to us.

So enjoy saving time. Enjoy happier clients. And enjoy your career getting prospects to make "yes" decisions.

About the Authors

Bernie De Souza coaches financial advisors and executives, and also conducts workshops for financial advisors and insurance agents. Topics include automatic referral systems, filling diaries with appointments, creating high-level networking events, prospecting for high-level clients and more.

As a keynote speaker, Bernie conducts entertaining presentations at company events and recently presented as a keynote speaker at the MDRT.

To contact Bernie,
call +44 1926 800163

Or email him at
Bernie@BernieDeSouza.com

Tom "Big Al" Schreiter conducts keynote presentations and live workshops on how the mind works, and how we can effectively get "yes" decisions.

To contact Tom,
call +1 281-280-9800

Or contact him through his website at
http://www.BigAlBooks.com

21494822R00082

Printed in Great Britain
by Amazon